THIS BOOK BELONGS

_____

INSERT PHOTO HERE

NAME:

1

INSERT PHOTO HERE

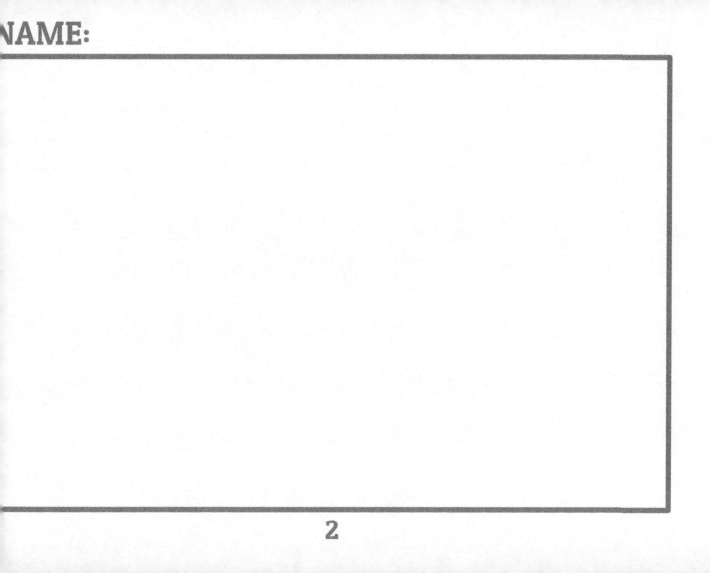

INSERT PHOTO HERE

NAME:

3

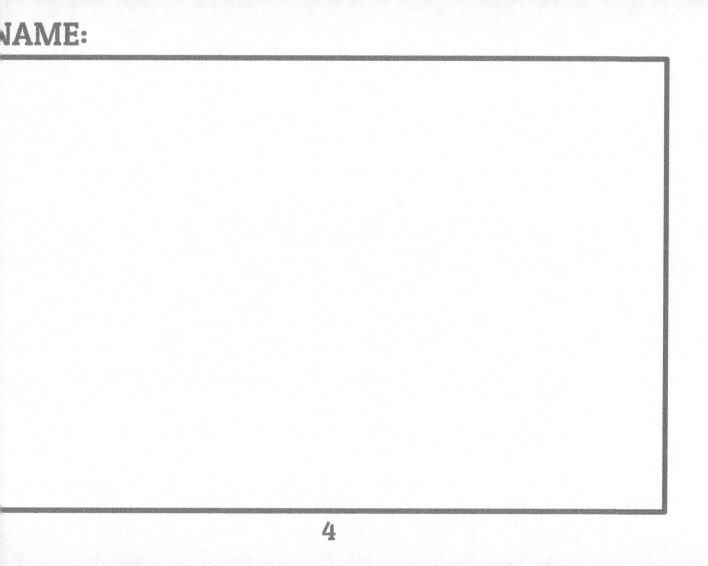

INSERT PHOTO HERE

NAME:

5

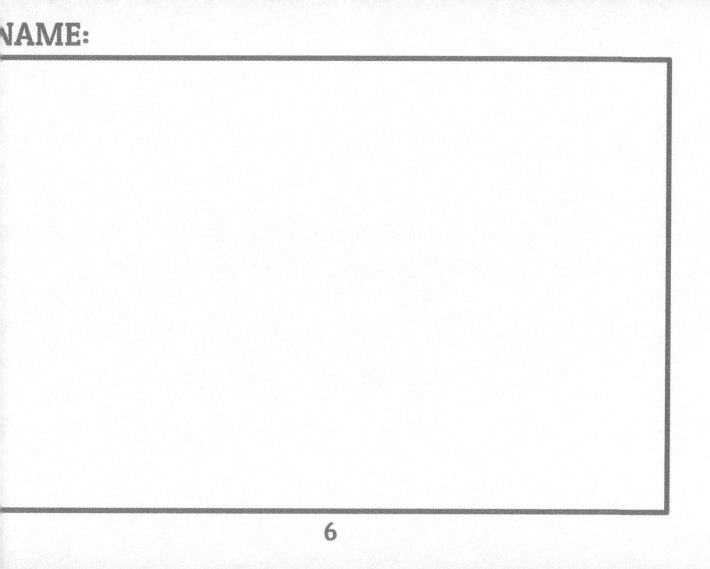

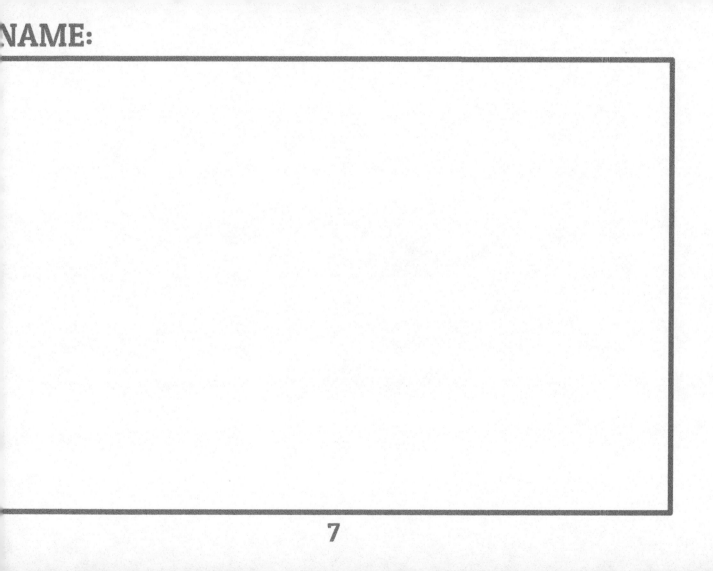

INSERT PHOTO HERE

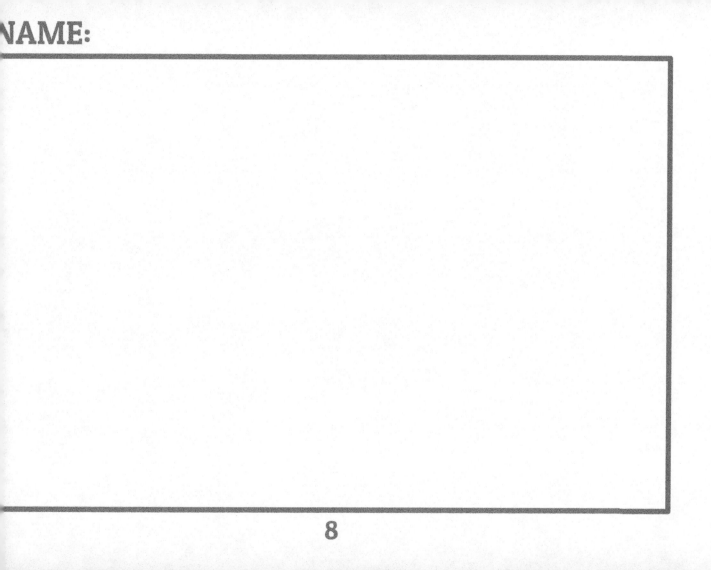

INSERT PHOTO HERE

NAME:

9

INSERT PHOTO HERE

NAME:

11

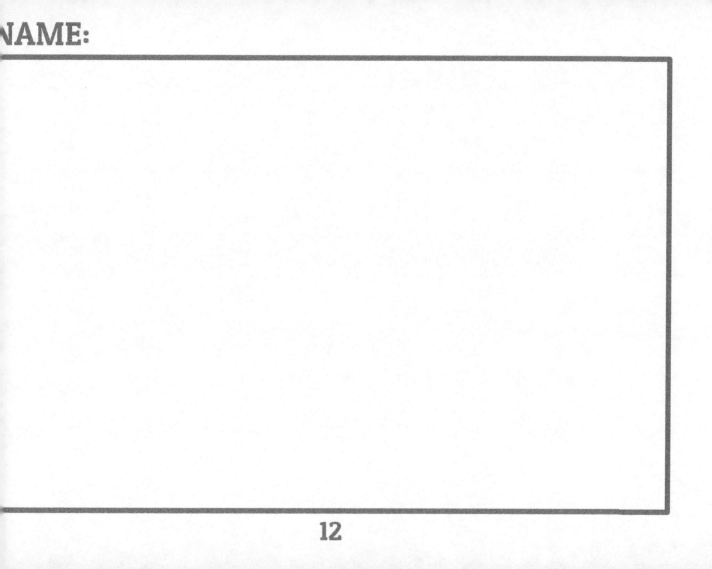

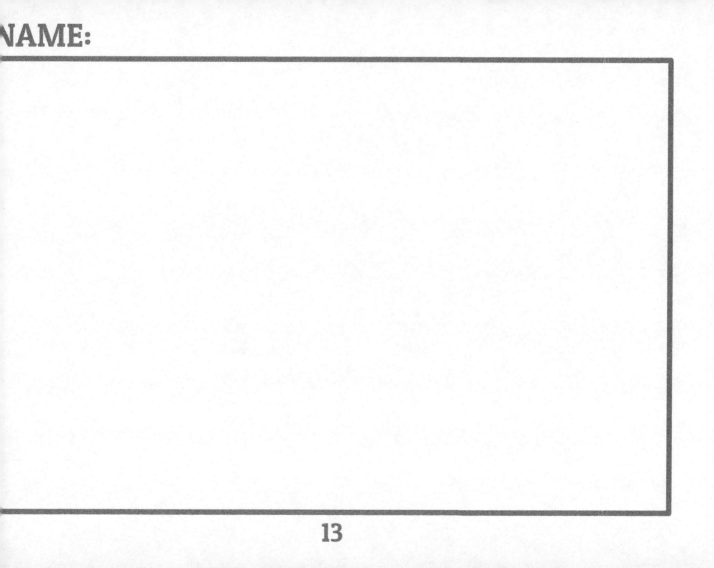

INSERT PHOTO HERE

NAME:

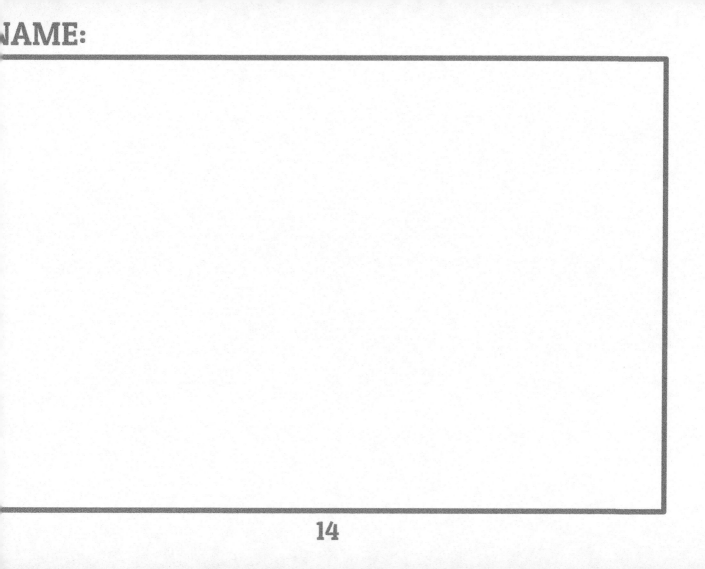

15

INSERT PHOTO HERE

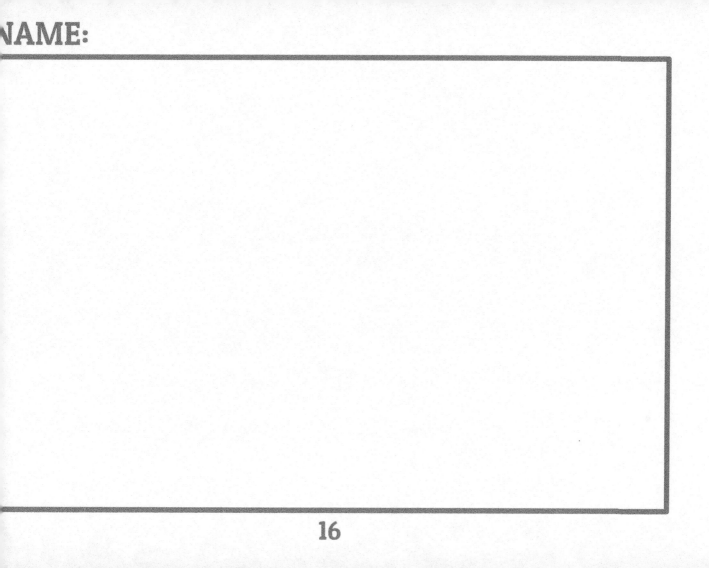

INSERT PHOTO HERE

NAME:

17

NAME:

INSERT PHOTO HERE

19

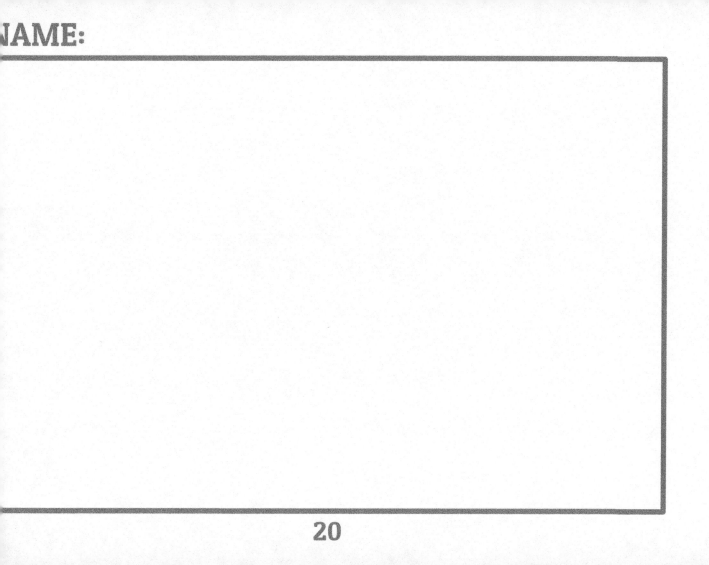

20

NAME:

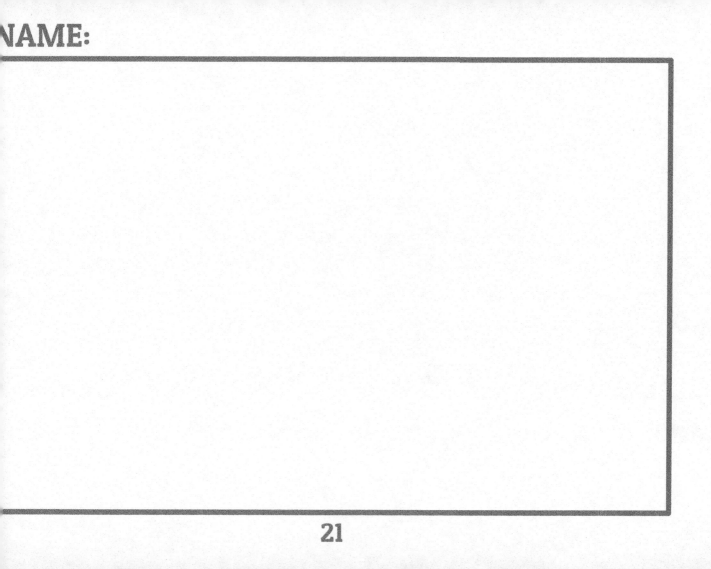

NAME:

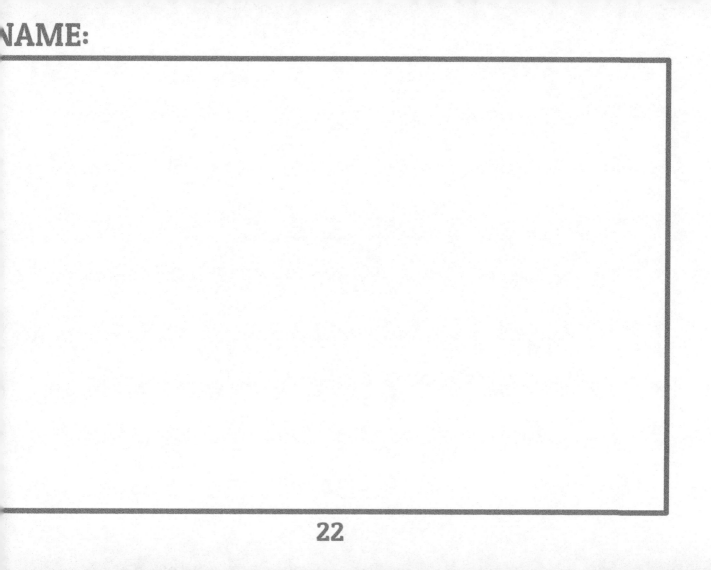

INSERT PHOTO HERE

NAME:

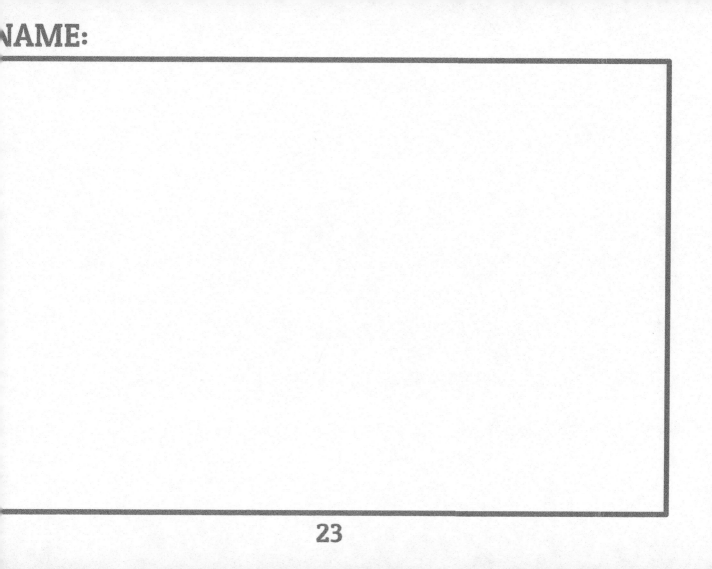

NAME:

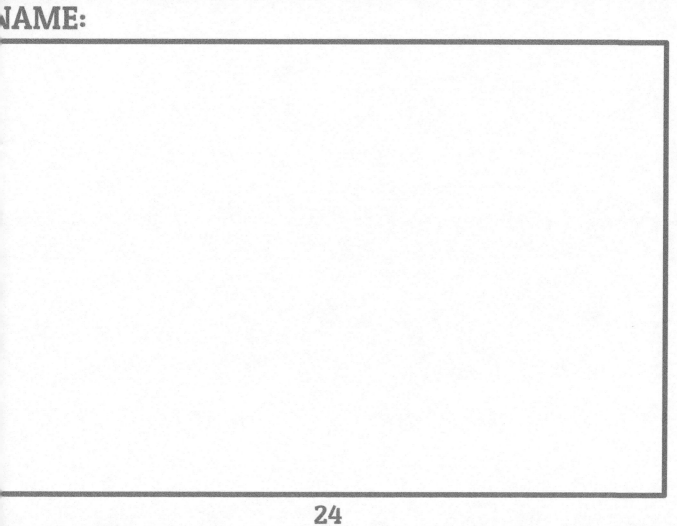

NAME:

25

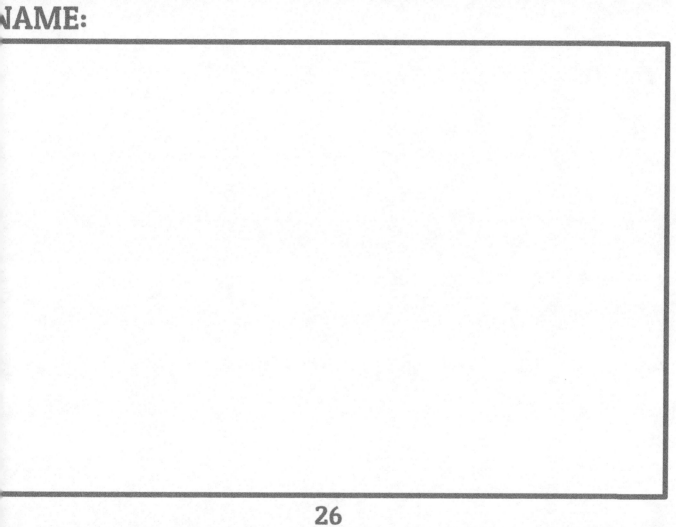

26

INSERT PHOTO HERE

NAME:

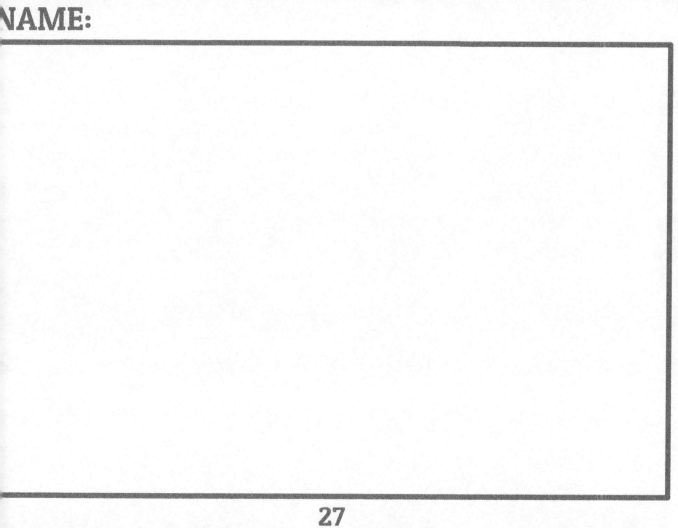

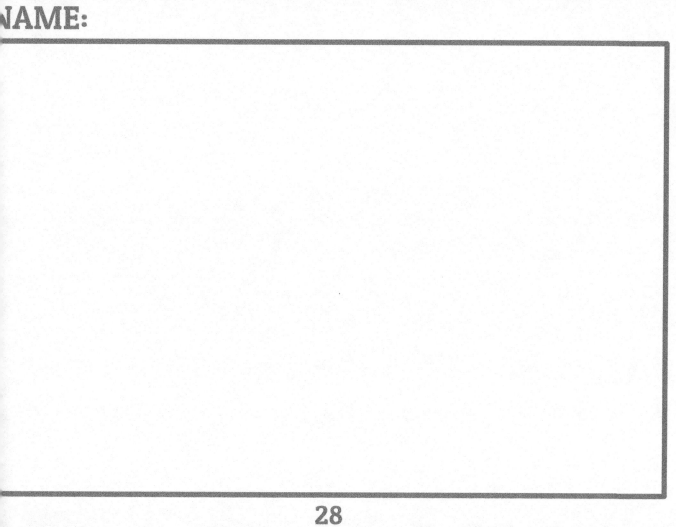

28

NAME:

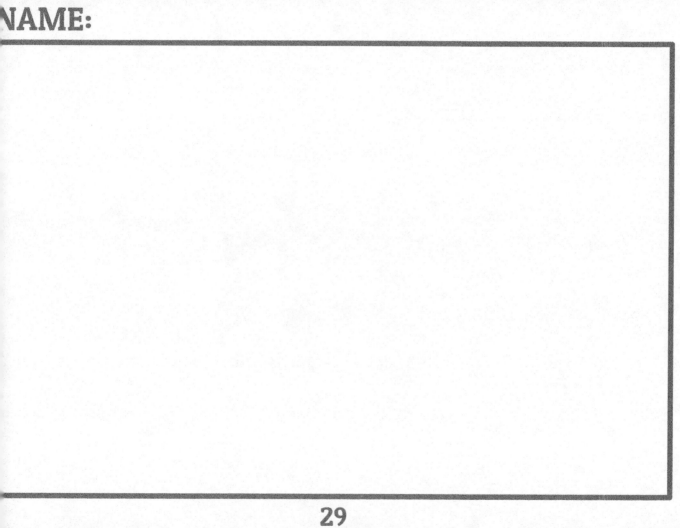

INSERT PHOTO HERE

NAME:

30

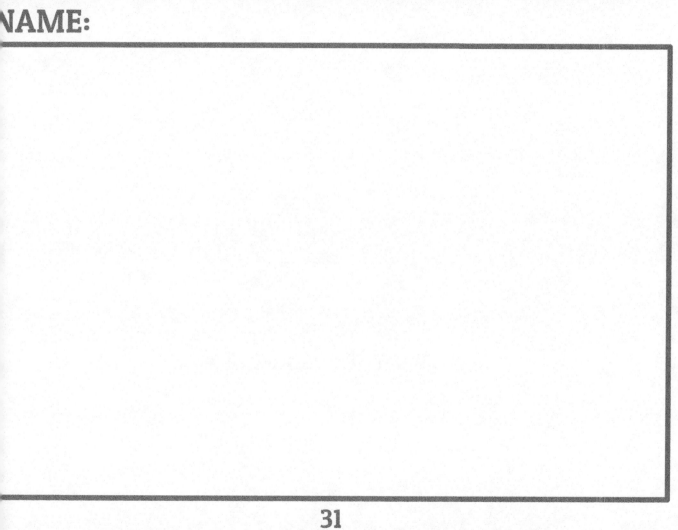

NAME:

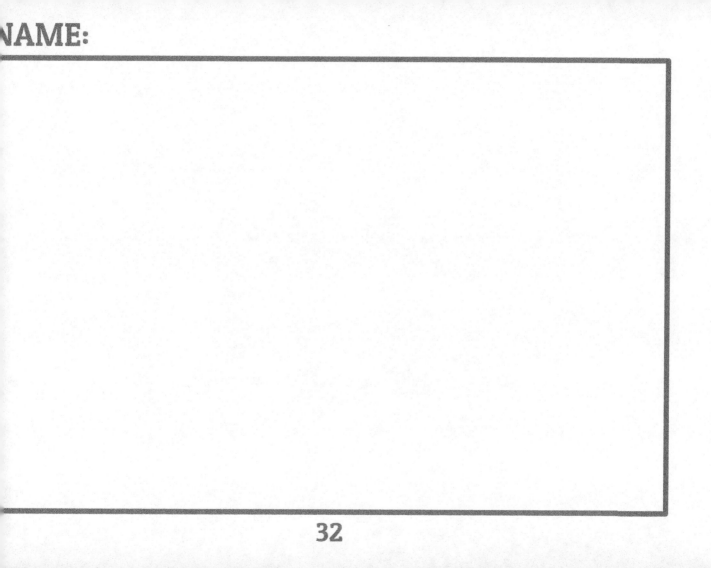

NAME:

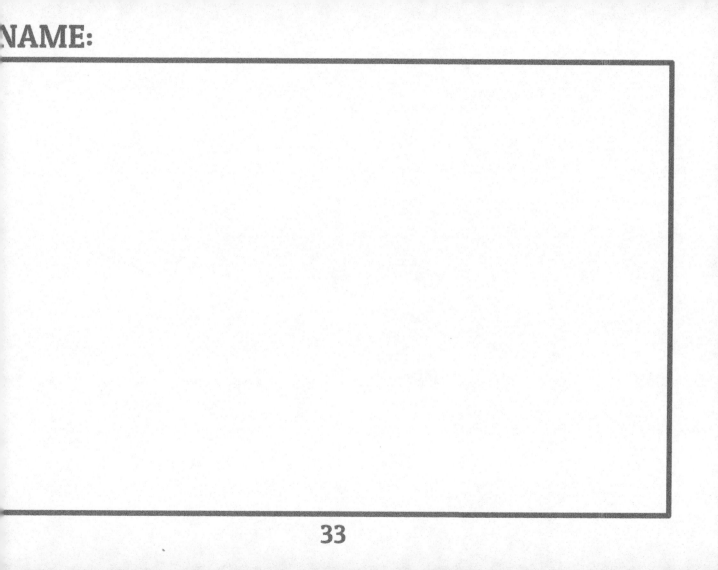

NAME:

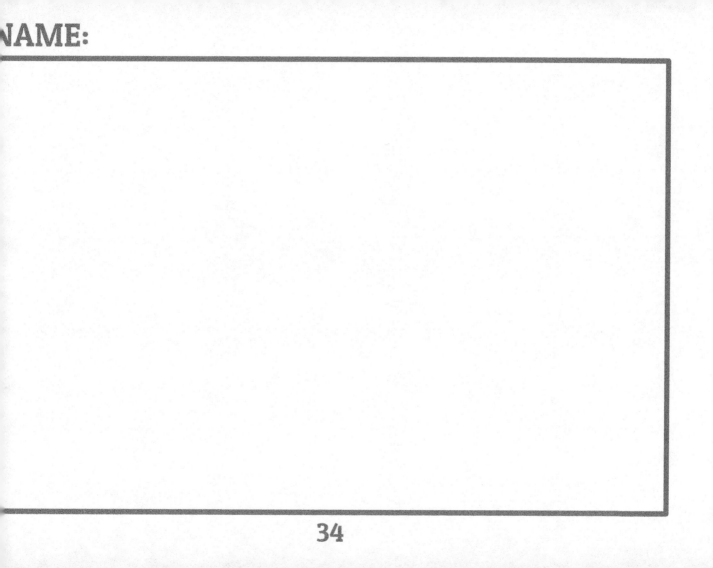

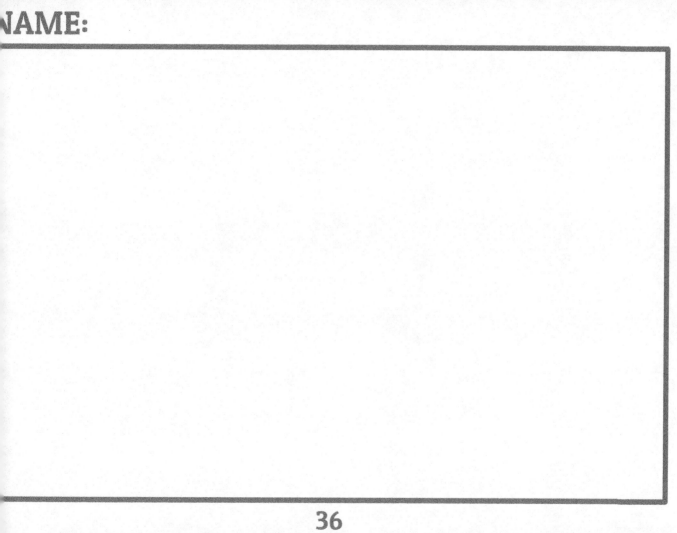

INSERT PHOTO HERE

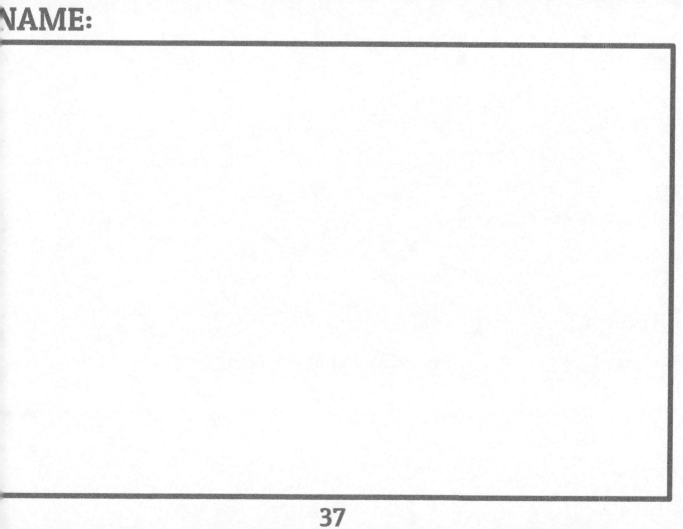

37

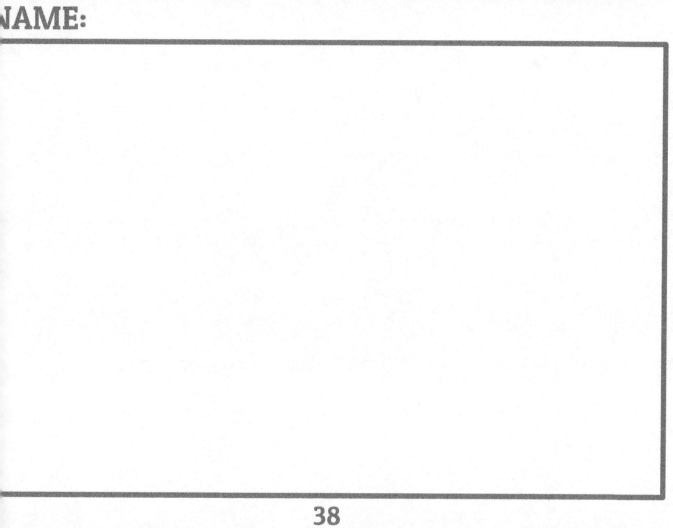

38

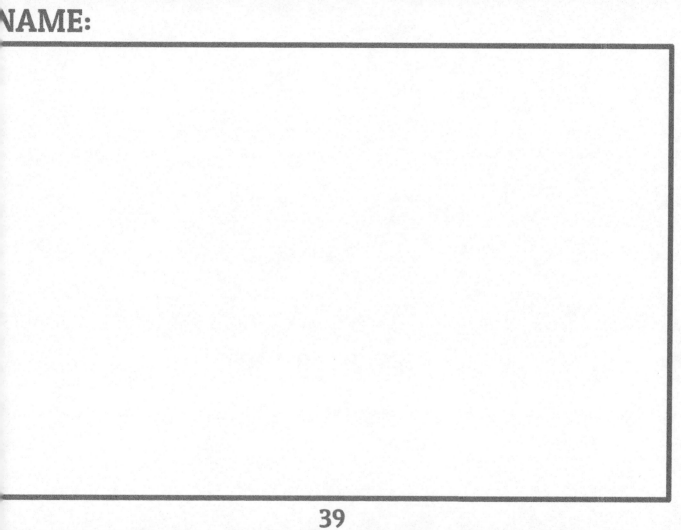

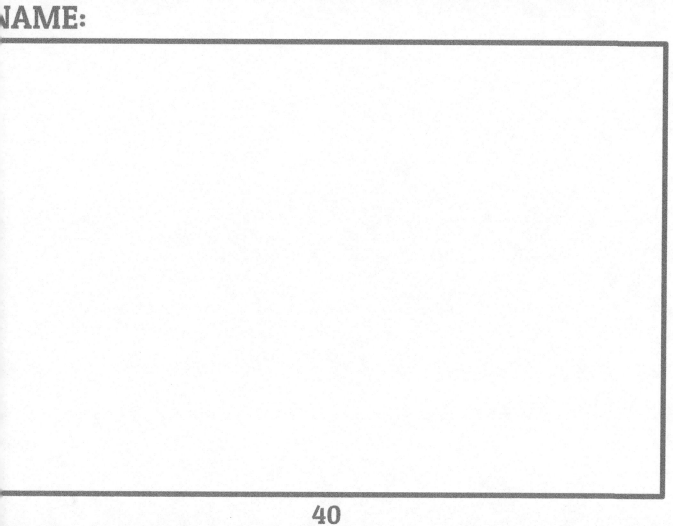

NAME:

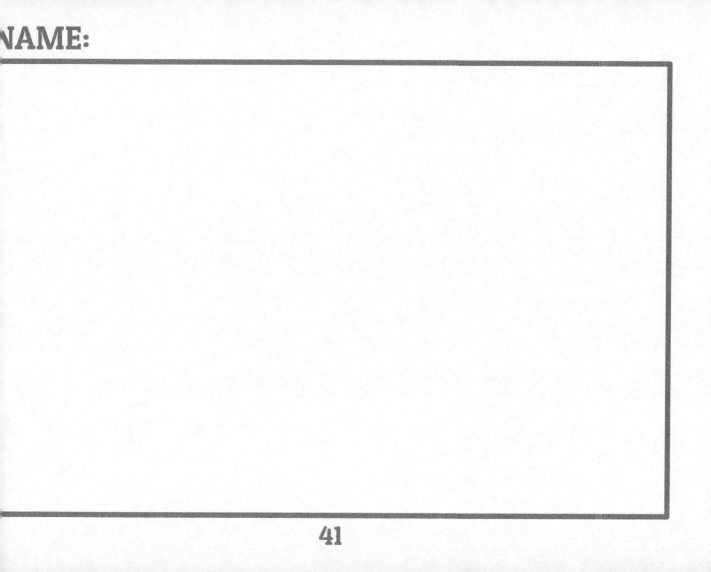

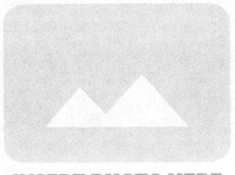

NAME:

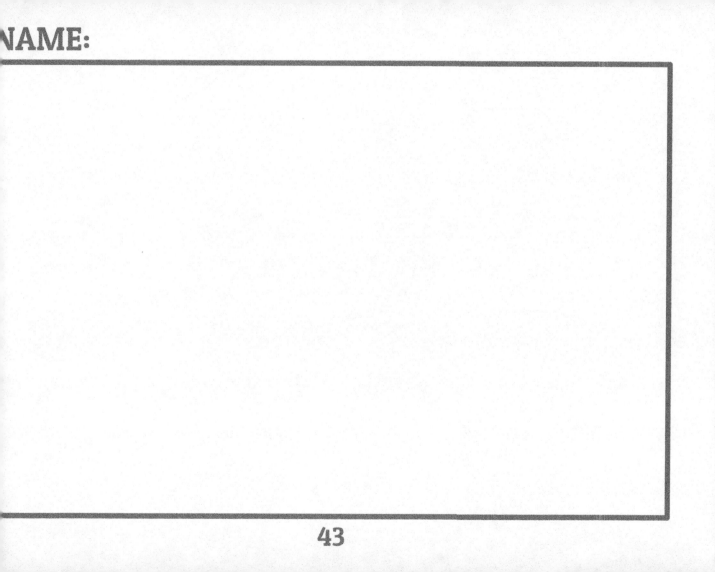

INSERT PHOTO HERE

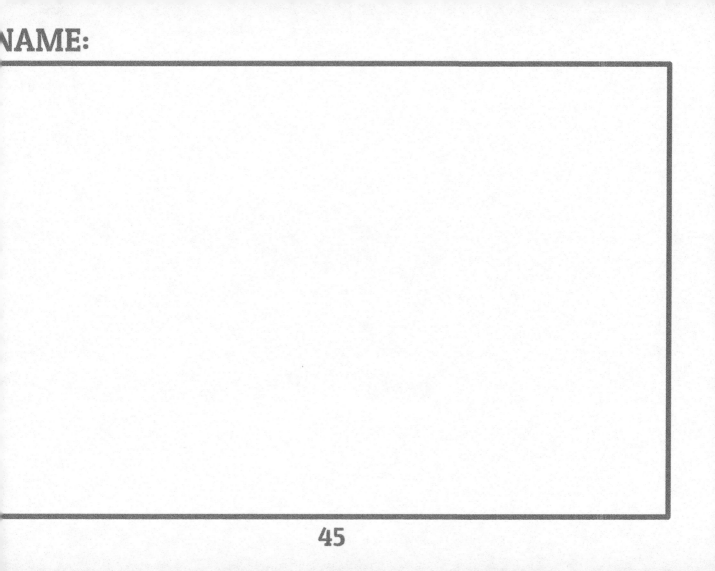

45

INSERT PHOTO HERE

NAME:

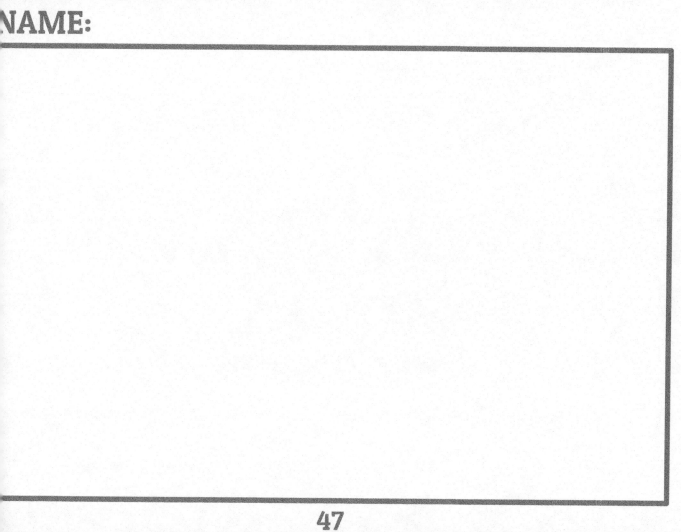

NAME:

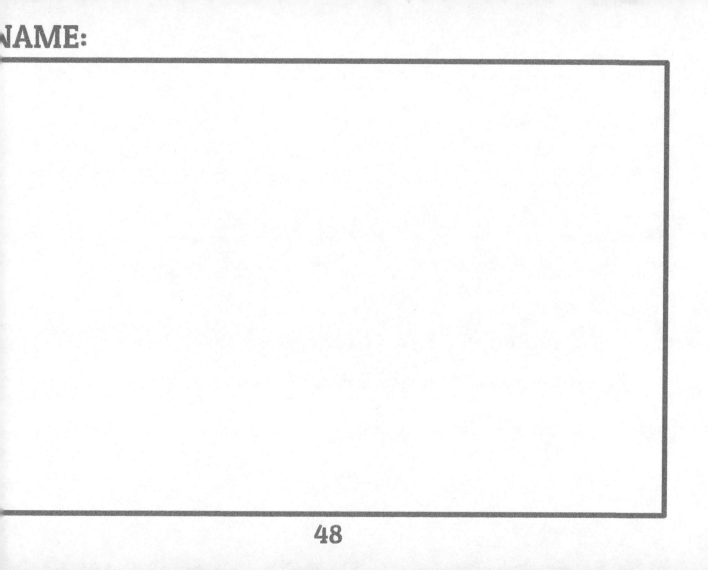

INSERT PHOTO HERE

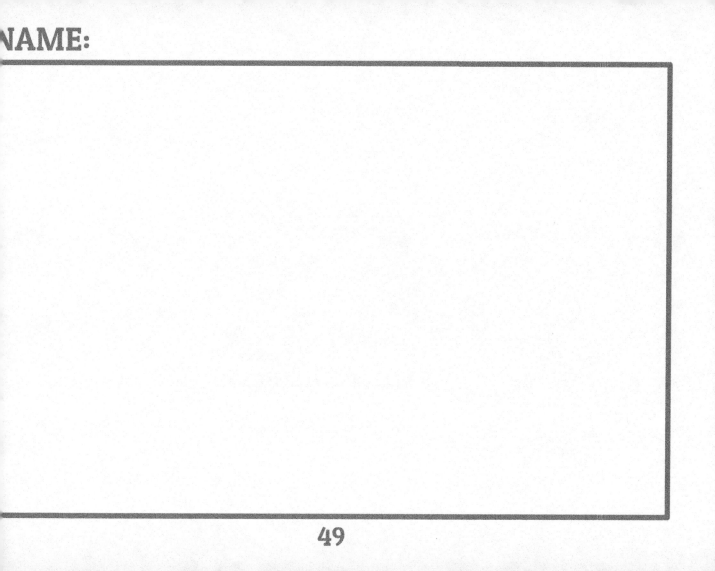

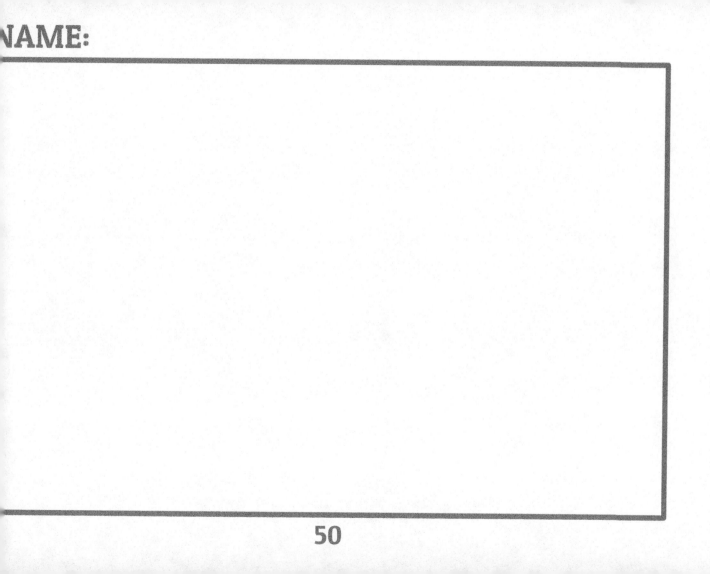

IMPRESSUM: STEVEN BLOOR
KÖNIGSBERGER STRAßE 13 | 23714 BAD MALENTE-GREMSMÜHLEN
TELEFON: 01520/4802343 | E-MAIL: info@blr-marketing.de

Made in the USA
Monee, IL
13 August 2024